Putting On Your Pantos

John Cooper

Illustrations by Haydn Cooper

An environmentally friendly book printed and bound in England by
www.printondemand-worldwide.com

Mixed Sources
Product group from well-managed forests, and other controlled sources
www.fsc.org Cert no. TT-COC-002641
© 1996 Forest Stewardship Council
FSC

PEFC Certified
This product is from sustainably managed forests and controlled sources
www.pefc.org
PEFC
PEFC/16-33-415

This book is made entirely of chain-of-custody materials

FastPrint Publishing

www.fast-print.net/store.php

Putting On Your Pantos

ISBN 978-178035-412-5

First published 2012 by
FASTPRINT PUBLISHING
Peterborough, England.

Contents

Cinderella

THE CAST

Cinderella	Young, beautiful and sexy – everything you wished your wife could be.
Sister One	Big, fat and smells of cabbage.
Sister Two	Younger and hairier than Sister One.
Baron	Mean, moody and moronic.
Fairy Godmother	An old crone, a bag lady – most of them under her eyes.

ACT ONE

Cinderella — My name is Cinderella
I'm sixteen years of age
I'm beautiful, slim and sexy,
And it makes my sisters rage.

Sister One — I'm Cinder's elder sister,
I like to call her Cind
I may be fat, but I smell nice,
Except when I break wind.

Sister Two — I'm the younger sister,
For our Prince I have a pash,
Some folks think I'm pretty,
It's a shame about the tash.

Cinderella — Now that we know one another,
I must tell you I'm feeling so sad,
I can't go to the ball tonight,
Because of my evil Dad.

Enter the Baron to hisses and boos.

Baron — Now is the winter of my discontent
This weather gives me the hump,
Cinders – get down and clean the floor,
This place is looking a dump.

Sister One		Oh Daddy dear, how witty you are,
Sometimes you send me in fits,
I laugh so much, my bra rides up
And makes me wiggle my – toes.

Cinderella		Please may I go to the ball tonight?
I love to dance and sing,
I want to be close to our handsome Prince,
I told you, I'm a sexy young thing.

Sister Two		No, you can't go to the ball tonight,
You'll stay here, there's things to be done,
We two will go and give them a treat,
We're built for all kinds of fun.

Baron		Now then dears, off you go,
When we're there, we'll have such a rave,
You have a bath, I'll have a shower,
And you number two, have a shave.

Baron and Sisters leave.

Cinderella		Now they have gone – I'm all alone,
I think that I'm going to cry,
It's times like this, you need a Godmother,
Where is she? Oh me, oh my. (Cry's)

Enter Godmother.

Godmother Here I am, sorry I'm late,
Just in time though to give you advice,
Pop out to the shops, come back soon,
Bringing a pumpkin and six white mice.

Cinderella What luck I bought these things earlier,
Here they are, show us what you can do,
Make me look sexy and raunchy,
Or it's the old people's home for you.

Godmother I call out the magic words,
I wave my magic wand,
Before you can say Jack Robinson,
Your mousy hair has turned blonde.

So like Tommy Cooper,
'Uh, Uh – just like that,'
A pair of crystal glass slippers,
A dress, and a matching hat.

Cinderella Thank you Fairy Godmother,
I hope I'm not overdressed,
For through this diaphanous blouse,
I think you can see my vest.

Godmother Off you go my child,
Your coach you must alight,
Remember, all turns back to tat
Exactly at midnight.

ACT TWO

The ball is over, and the Baron and the two Sisters are lounging around.

Baron	Oh what a rotten party, Eating trifle, custard and prunes, And such tatty decorations, With condoms being used as balloons. Nobody there to scrounge from, 'Round the bar, never seen such a crush, Oh no! those prunes are starting to work, Excuse me, I'll have to rush.

Baron exits – quickly.

Sister One	Who the hell was the flashy bird? With legs up to her armpits, Her bum leaving a lasting impression On cushions whenever she sits.
Sister Two	I don't know who she was, But His Majesty's eyes rolled in their sockets, He couldn't keep his ruddy hands still, And they were still in his pockets.

Enter Cinderella singing happily.

Cinderella	Ah, what a wonderful night it was,
I danced and shouted with glee,
And it was obvious from the way that he walked,
That the Prince was pleased to see me.

Sister One	Hey you, get back to your work!
Haven't you heard what's being said?
The Prince is bringing a glass slipper,
Who it fits is the one that he'll wed.

Sister Two	I think it's bound to be me,
About Princes, I sure know my onions,
If I squeeze just a little bit hard,
It might slip over my bunions.

Sister One	No such luck my hairy friend,
My feet are so much more dainty,
He'll like me, and I like him,
He sure is handsome, ain't he?

Sister Two	Out of the way, here he comes,
My knees have all turned to jelly,
The hairs on my body are beginning to rise,
Including the hairs on my Belly.

Cinderella — Isn't he wonderful,
Handsome, tall, elegant and lean?
And in that hose, he's so very well built,
I'm sure you know what I mean.

Sister One — Here Prince, try me first,
I'm sure that I'm the right size,
But if by chance, the shoe doesn't fit,
You're still in line for a prize.

Cinderella — Out of the way you silly girls,
Have a drink and eat a cookie,
For I'm the sexy little thing,
Who'll give the prince his nookie.

Enter the Baron and Godmother.

Baron — Girls, girls, look what I have found,
She could be the answer to my prayer,
She has loads of money,
I think I'm in lust with her.

Godmother — Oh foolish, foolish little man,
You can think just what you like
But you'll soon change your tiny mind
When you find out I'm a transvestite.

Cinderella *(To audience)* I'll get the Prince for sure,
All these will get their come-uppance,
Remember, stay sexy and raunchy,
But keep your hand over your tuppence.

END

Jack and the Beanstalk

THE CAST

Mother	A poor but lively widow, with all the desires of a younger woman.
Jack	A lonely lad, suspiciously too fond of the family cow. Spends too much time in his room.
Peeping Tom	Real name – Mister Bates, known as a boy as Master Bates. Has slowly fading eyesight.
Giant	The product of a broken marriage which turned him away from his love of crochet and morris dancing, into a pathological killer.
Goose	The young daughter of a good family who told a visiting gypsy to 'pee off'.

ACT ONE

Mother

Oh Jack, what can we do
We have no food to eat
Only old clothes on our back
And no shoes on our feet.

I really don't know what to do
I may have to sell my body,
When your father was alive
Sex was our only hobby.

Jack

Don't talk silly Mother,
Men have better things to do
Than trying to get excited
By an old crone such as you.

Our old cow Daisy's a better bet,
She'll make a bob or two
She gives milk every day,
And she's got a beautiful moo.

Mother

How dare you suggest that men
With her would prefer to sleep,
I may be old and wrinkled
But I do come pretty cheap.

Jack I didn't mean that Mother,
It's our cow that has to be sold,
I'll take her to the market place
And exchange her for some gold.

Then with all that money
Our debts will all be paid,
And if there's some left over
I think that I'll get laid.

Mother I feel so sorry for you
When I hear the plan you've hatched,
For without a regular girlfriend
You and Daisy have come quite attached.

Jack Think nothing of it Mother,
I must do what I must do,
And if cows are in demand
I'll come back and try to sell you.

Mother *(Laughs)* Off you go you little scamp,
Enough of your tomfooleries
Anymore of your cheek
And I'll kick you in the goulies.

Peeping Tom *(Thru' window)* Forgive me for looking in
I was hoping to get some thrills,
But from what I have overheard,
I could help you to pay your bills.

I'm looking to buy a cow,
One that looks like yours,
Tell me, could you wrap it?
It's a present for 'er indoors.

Mother — Who the blinking heck are you?
What's your name, and the reason why
You're looking at me through the window,
By the way – fasten up your fly.

Peeping Tom — My name Madam, is Peeping Tom,
To you, I'll make this confession
I like to ogle ladies,
In fact, it's my profession.

Jack — Enough of this, you dirty man,
You have looked, and you've had your fun,
Mother go and put the kettle on,
By the way Sir, your fly's still undone.

Mother exits.

Jack — Now, what will you offer for Daisy?
I warn you my acumen is quite astute,
We have to be talking big 'big money'
As we're in desperate need for the loot.

Peeping Tom Young Sir, we might have a problem,
In monetary terms, the well's dry,
You see, I don't have any money,
Hang on while I do up my fly.

Peeping Tom I have something better to offer,
An answer to all your dreams,
Not gold, not cash, nor jewels,
But a handful of magic beans.

Jack Who do you think you're fooling?
But I'll listen to what you say,
How can these beans possibly help me,
And if they can, just in what way?

Peeping Tom Simply plant them in your garden,
Add water, and then jump clear,
They'll shoot up just like a rocket,
And your worries will then disappear.

Up there in the sky close to heaven,
There's jewels and gold by the score,
Just climb up the beanstalk and get it,
But be quiet when you open the door.

There's a big fellow that lives there,
As big as the proverbial bog,
He bites the head off babies,
But he's supposed to be kind to his dog.

Jack	You're not going to scare me, So give me the beans and run, Take our cow before Mother comes back, Hang on – your fly's come undone.
Peeping Tom	Right Daisy, we're off now, There's your beans – where's my hat? Before I go, I'd like to ask you, Know any women worth looking at?
Jack	Sod off, you dirty lecher, Take our cow, and then be gone, Your chosen profession disgusts me, And your friggin' fly's still undone.

Peeping Tom leaves, Mother enters.

Mother	So, your friend has gone Jack, It's something I'm glad to see, For the way he looked through the window, I'm sure that he fancied me. How much has he given us, For Daisy, our beautiful cow? If he's left us sufficient, I'll pop down to Asda now.

Jack	Steady on there Mother,
Money's not everything you know,
He's given us some magic beans,
That in the garden I'll sow.

Mother	Beans! Beans! Did you say beans?
You're giving me the needle,
Who was the fellow that gave you them,
Was it Jeremy Beadle?

You stupid little pillock,
I'm going to disown you,
You'd better go out and earn some cash
Before this week is through.

ACT TWO

Giant	Fee, Fie, Foe, Fum,
That's all I get to say,
Every Christmas Pantomime,
Right through till the first of May.

God, I'm so terribly bored,
I wish that I was dead,
It's ages since I was horrible,
And bit off a baby's head.

Hang on just a minute,
What's that noise I heard?
Goosey take a gander,
Note that play on words.

Goose — *(Complaining)* Alright! Alright, it's me again,
He's wearing out my legs,
When I'm not playing watch-dog,
I'm laying him golden eggs.

Goose — *(To Jack)* Hello, Hello, who are you?
You're so handsome, not a bit ugly,
And something else that caught my eye,
Is that you fit those tights so snugly.

Jack — Hello Goose, you're very smart,
In no way are you dumb,
If I can have some golden eggs,
I can get back in with my Mum.

Goose — Hang on just a minute,
Handsome you may be,
But before you get any golden eggs,
You'll hear my sad story.

My real name is Gwendoline,
A Princess of the land,
I was kidnapped by an evil witch,
Who waved her magic wand.

She turned me into what you see,
A goose with feathers galore,
Then lost me in a game of cards,
To that huge thing next door.

Now I'm sad and lonely,
The Giant's an awful baddy,
All I want is to go home
And see my Mummy and Daddy.

All — Aaaahhhhhhhh.

Jack — Don't you worry, me Duck,
You can tell I'm a Derbyshire lad,
I'll take you away from all this,
Right back to your Mam and Dad.

Goose — Jack if you do that,
I'm only too happy to say,
If you can get these feathers off,
It could well be your lucky day.

Jack — First let's get rid of the Giant,
That's not going to be an easy bet,
I've only got a penknife,
Guns haven't been invented yet.

Goose	Why not leave him in there? And quietly away from him walk, When we get home to your place, We'll chop down this damn beanstalk.
Giant	*(From other room)* What's that noise in there? It's causing me alarm, Come in here, let me see you, You know I'll do you no harm. *(To audience)* You know me folks, And today I'm feeling lucky, It may be some pretty young thing, And I might get me some nookie. It's about time I had some, Here alone and no-one to play, Only a goose for company, And that looks more attractive each day.
Goose	Quick, Jack let's run from him, Before in this room he has looked, There's one thing that's for certain, This goose is not getting cooked.
Jack	Right then, let me lift you, Under my arm you can go, We'll climb down the beanstalk together, And rest at my house down below.

Giant Come here you two scoundrels,
If I catch you you're manhood's at risk
I'll pull off your danglies with one hand,
And push them down your throat with my fist.

Goose Hurry Jack, oh please hurry!
Climb down the tree like a goat,
For if he does what he says, I'll be sad,
And you'll have a lump in your throat.

Jack Climbing down stalks isn't easy,
Especially when using one hand,
I'll be glad when we get to the bottom,
And have both feet on firm land.

At last we've reached terra-firma,
Mother quickly, give me a chopper,
I'll cut this beanstalk to the ground,
And finish the Giant good and proper.

Mother Here you are Jack, cut it down,
Perhaps then we'll both call a truce,
I hope that you've brought us some money,
And not just this skinny old goose.

Jack TIMBER! There it goes,
The Giant has gone for good,
If nothing else comes out of this,
At least we won't want for wood.

Mother Goodness, look what's happened,
I think I'm losing my mind,
The goose's feathers have come off
And left a luscious bird behind.

Jack Mother, this is Gwendoline,
From now on I'll call her Gwen,
For we are going to be married,
As soon as she says when.

Gwen Oh Jack, we'll get married,
Little goslings will come home to roost,
Meanwhile, mind where you're putting your hand,
'Cos I'm certain I've just been goosed.

END

Dick Whittington

THE CAST

Mother	A woman who looks like a pantomime Dame.
Dick	A naïve lad – the sort of person who tucks his shirt inside his underpants.
King	He has only a small part – one of the reasons why the Queen left him.
Princess	Young – attractive – innocent – boring.
Buggary Bob	A lecherous reprobate – every young girl has an uncle just like him.

ACT ONE

Scene – Mrs. Whittington's Garden.

Mother — Dick, Dick, where are you?
Come here you lazy slob,
Why don't you do as everyone else?
And get yourself a job?

Dick, Dick! – just hear me,
A more stupid name you'll not find.
When his father and me named him,
I can't think what I'd got on my mind.

Dick — Here I am darling Mother,
I was busy feeding the cat,
I think he may be having kittens,
What do you think of that?

Mother — Dick – sometimes you worry me,
After all you are twenty one,
Your cat's a he, not a ruddy she,
That's why we called it Tom.

Dick — I'm not sure that I understand you,
The details are not totally clear,
But I've seen him tending his private things,
Those at the front and the rear.

I've tried to stop him doing it,
It's something he really should quell,
It sets a bad example to children,
And I'm sure it makes his breath smell.

Mother — Never mind that Dick Whittington,
For you a job we must find,
There's rent to pay and food to buy,
So get off your fat behind.

Dick — I've looked everywhere Mother,
Don't be such an oppressor,
The trouble is as you know well,
No-one wants a ladies hairdresser.

Mother — Why can't you be more like your brother?
Get away from the hoi palloi
I think he's something in property
As in London he's called a rent boy.

I don't know exactly what's involved,
But it's done on quite a big scale,
At least, when I asked him about it,
He said it was to do with – wholesale.

Dick — I'll try anything Mother,
I'll work for hours and hours,
I'll give anyone ballet lessons,
Read poetry, or arrange flowers.

I could be an artist's model,
Or beautiful things I could paint,
But the thought of real hard work,
Makes me come over quite faint.

Enter Buggary Bob.

Buggary Bob My name is Buggary Bob,
Nicknamed from my time at sea,
Many a fresh faced cabin boy
Has received satisfaction from me.

I'm always ready for young chaps like you,
Or any experienced old Queen,
I come armed with my own golden rivet,
As well as my own Vasaline.

Mother Hang on, hang on you dirty old man,
Your unwanted attentions must stop,
My son will soon be a full grown man,
As soon as his danglies drop.

Dick What are you saying dear Mother?
Your course talk I don't understand,
And while we're on the subject of sex,
What has that man got in his hand?

Buggary Bob   Don't worry about this lad,
I'll put it away while we chat,
And if you still show no interest,
I'll have to make do with your cat.

Mother   Just you leave the lad alone,
All he wants is a job,
Anything else you've got in mind,
Is going to cost a few bob.

He's still young and innocent,
Good looking with no sign of fat,
Which makes it all the more galling,
To hear that you're eyeing the cat.

Dick   That's it Mother – I'm leaving,
I'll walk to London City,
And if you take exception to that,
Then Mother, that's really tough tittie.

Mother   No, no Dick don't leave me,
A poor widow woman all alone,
No men about the house,
And I'm not even on the phone.

Buggary Bob   I'll look after him missus,
I know the city quite well,
If we should run short of money,
His assets, we'll have to sell.

Mother — He doesn't need your company,
My attention is what he gets,
Keep away from his valuables,
His assets – or any other ets.

Buggary Bob — So be it, let the three of us go,
In London we'll find fortune and fame,
And if it all doesn't work out,
You'll have to go on the game.

Dick — Don't worry about it Mother,
I'm sure it won't come to that,
But if it came to making a choice,
We'll probably get more for the cat.

Mother — Get off with you, you silly young monkey,
Or I'll let Buggary Bob have his way,
That will wipe the smile off your face,
And you won't walk straight for a day.

Buggary Bob — Right then, let's be going,
To London with minimum fuss,
And as we are in a hurry,
Let's catch the sixty nine bus.

All — Hurrah!

ACT TWO

Scene – Streets of London.

Dick

I'm fed up with this,
I wish we'd never came,
To the town of London,
To find our fortune and fame.

Three months now we've looked for work,
And not yet had a sniff,
And whatever I've just trod in,
Gives off a hell of a whiff.

Buggary Bob

Why don't you shut up moaning?
You're going on far too long,
If you wipe your feet on the cat,
You might get rid of that pong.

Should that not do the trick,
I'll tell you something brother,
It's not the crap on your shoe that smells,
It's probably your Mother.

Mother

Hang on you foul mouthed git,
There's something you should know,
It can't be me that smells so bad,
I washed two months ago.

Anyway I say let's go,
Back to old chez repose,
For London as well as that horrible smell,
Is getting right up my nose.

Buggary Bob Right then, let us all make tracks,
I'll look up some of my chums
For I am very partial to,
Friendly deadbeats, hobos and bums.

Dick I like your naughty play on words,
But please just shut your gob,
For now is the time for us to leave,
That's Mum, me, the cat, and Bob.

Buggary Bob Just listen to those bloody bells
It's just as though they're talking,
I think they're trying to speak to us,
But ignore them, keep on walking.

Dick Stop and wait just a minute,
Can't you hear it everyone?
They're ringing out the message,
'Return Dick Whittington'

Mother I'm sure that it's a good omen,
Maybe someone has answered my prayer,
And if we go back to London Town,
Dick you'll become the Lord Mayor.

Buggary Bob Now then, who's this coming?
They're looking for you Dick and Tom,
And look at the beautiful girl with him,
I wouldn't mind giving her one.

Enter the King and Princess.

King Hello there, you won't know me,
See this crown and diamond ring?
That's because I rule this place,
And you may call me … King.

I'm looking all over London,
For anyone who might own cats,
I will grant them any wish,
If they'll get rid of the rats.

Dick That will be no trouble Sire,
Just leave it to Tom and me,
And when we've cleared this place of rats,
I will join your family.

Bob and Mum have taught me things,
Things that make the nights shorter,
And I shall try all of them,
When I'm married to your daughter.

Princess	What an uncouth young man, The worst that's past my eyes, Even if he kills the rats, He'll not get my bodily prize
King	I'm sorry Dear, I've given my word, We must all do our little bit, Should he rid the town of rats, I'm afraid you'll have to lump it.
Mother	That's right love, it's only fair, And though sexually he's not well blessed, Look upon the bright side, At least you'll get your hair dressed.
Buggary Bob	I know I'm old enough to be his Dad, But in the size department I shine, If you don't want to handle his small goods, You can always fondle mine.
Princess	I can't think of anything more horrid, But I'll do as my Father insists, If you Dick kill all of the rats, You can play with my wobbly bits.
Dick	I'm going now, come on Tom, No time to lose, let's run, The sooner we get rid of the rats, The sooner we both get some fun.

Later – In the Palace.

Mother	They've been gone two weeks now, I'm really worried sick, I think an awful lot of that cat, And quite a bit of Dick.
Princess	I've been thinking about him, And how they're getting on, For when he returns we'll be married, And I'll be Mrs. Whittington.
King	While I can't say that I've missed the lad, Or even his cat named Tom, What I have come to appreciate, Is the company of his Mum.
Mother	Why thank you very much Sire, My body, also yearns for you, It's been so long since I've been with a man, I've almost forgot what to do.
Princess	Wouldn't it be wonderful, If you Dad, Dick and me, Were married as a foursome, In one big ceremony.

Buggary Bob — This sloppy talk of weddings,
Is making me feel quite bad,
I'd much rather stay single,
And romp with a girl....or a lad.

King — Listen ! I hear someone coming,
I wonder if it's Dick,
Along with his faithful cat Tom,
I do hope they've done the trick.

Enter Dick and the cat.

Dick — Hello there everybody,
I'm sorry we've been so long,
We've been catching rats in the sewers,
I apologise for the pong.

Princess — Never mind that now darling,
It doesn't bother me, I swear,
For we are going to be married,
When Daddy has made you Lord Mayor.

King — Here Dick, is your chain of office,
Take it and please don't blush,
I promise that I won't pull it,
Just in case it makes you flush.

Mother Dick I'm so very proud of you,
And I'll tell you one more thing my lad,
About this time next Saturday,
The King here, will be your Dad.

Dick That's wonderful news Mother,
I feel absolutely grand,
Shame Bob will get no pleasure,
Unless he takes himself in hand.

Buggary Bob Don't worry about me sunshine,
I'll be alright, be sure of that,
For I want to announce my engagement,
To your faithful friend… Tom the cat.

All Hurrah !

END

Snow White and the Other Seven Dwarfs

THE CAST

Snow White	Young and beautiful – and knows it.
Queen	Wicked, yet attractive, in a Barbara Cartland sort of way.
Prince	A poseur. Feather in the hat, tight hose. Measures his intellect in inches.
Dwarfs	Snooty – Although only 3'-0" high, thinks he's above everyone.
	Nosey – Gets up everyone elses with all his questions.
	Drippy – Has a water works problem.
	Dopey – Always high, but not in stature.
	Randy – A groper. Has a vivid imagina tion, and failing eye sight.
	Windy – A walking advert for baked beans.
	Kevin – The odd one out.
Mirror	(Voice only) Not a patch on The Sun.

ACT ONE

Scene opens in the Queen's Palace.

Queen	Mirror, Mirror on the wall, Tell me honestly, Who is the fairest of them all, Young Snow White, or me? I may be a little bit older, But my body is curvy and firm I also have vast experience, And what I don't know, I'll learn. All that I have is genuine, No implants of Silicone, Everything that you see that wobbles, Is all of my very own. Now then Mirror, tell the truth, As long as it's me that you class, As the most beautiful woman, Or we're likely to hear broken glass.
Mirror	The question you pose is quite tricky, As your Highness needs to be flattered, But if I'm to tell the truth, We're both likely to be shattered.

Here goes, this is it,
Your Highness there is no disgrace,
But when compared with Snow White,
Your beauty takes second place.

Queen — Mirror, Mirror on the wall,
On your answer, I will spit,
You may wish to re-consider,
When you've reflected on it.

Enter Snow White.

Snow White — Hello Step-Mummy darling,
My word you do look mad,
Have you had an argument
With my dearest darling Dad?

I am feeling wonderful,
My hair has a beautiful sheen,
My eyes are bright, my teeth are white,
And what's more, I'm just seventeen.

Everyone thinks I'm lovely,
And says how glamorous I am,
All of the men lust after me,
Like they did with Princess Diane.

Queen Spare me all the details,
I'm so full of malice,
That I'm inclined to banish you,
From the Royal Palace.

In fact, that's what I'll do,
I can do anything that I like,
So pack your bags, get out of here,
In other words-'On yer bike'.

Snow White Oh you are beastly to me,
I've no-where else to go,
It was probably you that gave me
The ridiculous first name – Snow.

Anyway I can't go yet,
There's something I'm waiting upon,
I've ordered my meat from the Butcher,
And some day my mince will come.

Queen With horrible puns like that one,
You will be banished to the wood,
Then I'm going to make sure,
When you've gone, you're gone for good.

Then while out there you will die,
Perhaps by your own hand,
Then I will be the undisputed,
Most beautiful woman in the land.

Scene changes to woodland, with Snow White asleep.

Dwarfs enter, singing.

Dwarfs

Hi Ho, Hi Ho,
We're seven Dwarfs you know,
We're not deformed,
But perfectly formed,
From head to toe, Hi Ho

Hi Ho, Hi Ho,
Into the woods we go,
We'll find a girl,
And have a whirl,
Then things will grow, Hi Ho,

Hi Ho, Hi Ho,
We're not queer you know,
The company we keep,
Includes dogs and sheep,
And the occasional pro. Hi Ho,

Och Hi, Och Hi,
We're only three feet high,
We put on stilts,
To wear our kilts,
With a velcro fly, Hi Ho,

Hi... *(Kevin interrupts)*

Kevin Scccchh, quiet everybody,
There's a girl asleep over there,
She's gorgeous just to look at,
With her shiny jet black hair.

Randy Where? Where? Let me see,
Out of my way I beg,
It's absolutely ages since
I've seen a decent leg.

Dopey Wow man, she's just great,
Lying there in these glades,
Hold this joint, I'll get a better look,
When I've taken off my shades.

Drippy I'd like to take a look,
But I'm afraid as you all know,
That as soon as I get excited,
I really have to... go.

Snooty You six Dwarfs make me sick,
That girl there lying on the grass,
Is obviously some-one special
And way out of your class.

Nosey What do you mean – special?
Is she a Princess or even a Queen?
And as she's lying around in the woods,
Where do you think she's been?

Windy	I think she's wonderful, Lying there under that tree, Oops, sorry everybody, The smell is coming from me.
Snow White	*(Waking)* Oh my… who are you? I'm so startled that I may cry, Seeing the seven of you standing there, With the tallest only four foot high.
Snooty	Let me introduce myself, I'm Snooty, and far superior To all the other Dwarfs, Who can kiss my fat posterior.
Nosey	Who are you, and what's your name? How tall, how short, how long? You see why they call me Nosey, As the questions roll off my tongue.
Drippy	My name is Drippy, A name I heartily resent, It's only because of my prostate, That I'm so incontinent.
Randy	My name is Randy, Because I'm a real pervert, I like to look down blouses, Or even up a skirt.

Dopey	Hi man, give me five, Dopey is my name, If you want to smoke some grass, Then Baby I'm always game.
Kevin	My name is Kevin, How boring you may cry, No-one remembers who I am, As my name doesn't end in a Y.
Windy	People call me Windy, Please don't take offence, For I have a problem, With embarrassing flatulence.
Snow White	That's alright, don't be shy, For though I'm virginal and pure, If I have baked beans for my tea, It'll happen to me, for sure. Now that we know each other, My sad tale I will uncover, I've been abandoned in these woods, On the orders of my wicked Step-Mother. She's so jealous of my looks, She's left me here to die, Then she'll be the fairest in the land, Hold on lads… I'm going to cry.

Randy — There, there, wipe your eyes,
There's no need to make a fuss,
Let me put my arm around you,
Then you can come home with us.

Snooty — Leave her alone you lecher
Your hands you must not let roam,
Or she will be too frightened,
To come with us to our home.

Snow White — Thank you so much everyone,
To join you will be a delight,
And I will help in any way,
Or my name is not Snow White.

Dopey — I'll snort to that Baby,
Our pad will jump and jive,
You can take some ecstasy,
And be glad that you're alive.

Nosey — Hang on just a moment,
There's a question I want to present,
Has she got any money
To pay her share of the rent?

Kevin — Nosey, there's no need for that,
Snow White your welcome to come back,
We can have fun train spotting,
If you've got an anorak.

Snow White I'd love to do that Kevin,
I wish you could see my chums,
I've sent a film to be developed,
To get snaps for our albums.

The films they went to the chemist,
So it's Boots they're coming from,
You all will have to be patient,
For one day my prints will come.

Randy If it's photographs that you want,
I've got some with me and a girl,
In poses so explicit,
They'll make your toe-nails curl.

Drippy Out of the way you pervert,
Remember, she's the King's Daughter,
Your lewd talk could cause offence,
Hang on – I must pass water.

Windy Carry on Drippy, I'll have a say,
With your comments I agree,
Randy you are objectionable,
Oops sorry – that was me.

Snooty Come on everyone,
Back to the cottage we'll go,
There we will have a nice cup of tea,
If that's alright with you Snow.

Snow White — That's a wonderful idea,
We'll tell jokes and have a good laugh,
I'll sing and dance and look pretty,
In fact, be irritatingly naff.

Scene changes to the Dwarfs House, where Snow White is ironing clothes.

Enter the Queen.

Queen — Hello there my Darling,
It's ages since we saw each other,
I hope that you don't bear a grudge
Against your dearest Mother.

Snow White — Why Mother, how dare you come
And disturb me in my new home,
After you jealously abandoned me,
In the woods, helpless and alone.

Queen — There, there, please forgive me,
The reasons are difficult to grapple,
Some day I'm sure you'll understand,
In the meantime, take this apple.

I've brought it specially for you,
It's such a beautiful red,
It will help you dream of your Prince,
As you lie here in your bed.

Snow White Well, well, that is a surprise,
And so I thank you Mater,
But if it's alright with you,
I'll eat the apple later.

Queen No, no, of course my dear,
I'll go now, and happy dreams,
(Aside) When she's eaten the apple,
It will end my wicked schemes.

The Queen leaves, laughing.

Snow White *(Bites apple)* Mmm, this is lovely,
I'll rest awhile and convince
Myself that in the near future,
I shall meet my handsome Prince.

He'll ask me to marry him,
… I've suddenly gone quite drowsy,
What's more this rosy apple,
Tastes absolutely lousy.

Snow White collapses.

Dwarfs enter, singing.

Dwarfs	Hi Ho, Hi Ho, It's back home we go, And there en-masse, We'll all harass Our beautiful Snow.
Snooty	Hold on! Be quiet! She's lying here by the bed, I hope she's only sleeping, And not so tragically dead.
Nosey	Here! Let me look, Let me get close I insist, For I can see inside her mouth, There's a piece of Granny Smiths.
Windy	Apples tend to give me the wind, But as I've often said, Flatulence may be embarrassing, But it's better than being dead.
Drippy	Don't be so morbid Windy, She's only asleep, you'll see, All this excitement is too much, I'll have to go and have a Pee.

Dopey — Respect man, respect due,
To Snow White and all her folk,
Now if you'll all excuse me,
I'm going to snort some coke.

Randy — If Snow White should be dead,
It will cause us all great consternation
Therefore please let me be the one
To give mouth to mouth resuscitation.

Kevin — Keep away from her you sod,
As your attention only brings
Embarrassment, as you always try
To put your hands on her....things.

Snooty — Quiet, there's someone approaching,
He's tall and so well dressed,
He's obviously from a good family,
I have to say I'm impressed.

Clear the way everybody,
Let the gentleman through,
You can easily tell from his bearing,
That his blood just has to be blue.

Enter the Prince.

Prince | Hello, I'm the Prince of this land,
The castle over there's my address.
When I'm not slaying dragons,
I'm saving young ladies in distress.

As you can see I'm right handsome,
From my toes to the top of my head,
I'm brave, I'm bold – a real smoothy,
What's more, I'm damned good in bed.

Dopey | Hold on there now big Brother,
Excuse us for making a fuss,
But our friend has just passed away,
O.D'd on a Golden Delicious.

Kevin | That's right Dopey, you tell him,
In fact in the argument I'll join,
For Prince or no Prince, if you talk like that,
I'll head-butt you right in the groin.

Prince | Sorry, I didn't mean to upset you,
Your sorrow is easy to tell,
I'll take a closer look at her,
By the way, what's that awful smell?

Windy | I'm sorry about that everyone,
I'm in need of hot water and towels,
All of this has upset me so much,
I'm losing control of my bowels.

Prince I'll take her in my manly arms,
Her heart will start to flutter,
The apple that lies within her mouth,
Will melt like Danish butter.

Drippy Hurry now, please be quick,
I'm afraid you'll have to rush,
While you're doing that small thing,
I'll nip behind this bush.

Snooty Look, the apples fallen out,
Her cheeks have a bright patina,
I really must get a grip of myself,
As I'm losing my demeanour.

Randy Yes, she is stirring now,
Her young breasts falling and rising,
That's not all that's coming up,
Which no-one finds surprising.

Kevin Not from you, anyway,
But she is beginning to stir,
Move back everybody
And give Snow White some air.

Nosey Right Prince, the apple's gone,
But where did you get your knowledge?
Was it at medical school,
Or an agricultural college?

Prince — Now that you're fully awake,
Your eyes look so much bigger,
Let me help you to your feet,
Then I can admire your figure.

Snow White — Oh my, how good looking you are,
My heart is beating and thumping,
And from the strange feelings I have,
You've started my oestrogen pumping.

Prince — What a figure, what a face,
What hips, what waist, what bust,
I'm getting so excited,
I think I've fallen in lust.

Marry me, oh sweet Snow White,
Please be my blushing bride,
I can hardly contain myself,
'Till you're lying by my side.

Snow White — Prince Charming we'll get married,
Ring the bells boys, bang the drum,
I can see from the front of his hose,
That at last – my Prince has come.

END

Sleeping Beauty

THE CAST

King Tallia	Gets his excitement single-handed.
Princess Jenny Tallia	A private person.
Wicked Queen	A man hater.
Mother Plucker	Widowed mother of Jack.
Idle Jack	Gardener, but can't tell his larch from elder.
Prince Percy Vere	A real trier.

ACT ONE

The scene opens in the King's Castle with Mother Plucker, who cleans and cooks for the Royal Family, dusting the furniture.

Mother P

Hello there every body,
I hope you know my name,
For in this years Pantomime
I'm the one that plays the Dame

People call me Mother Plucker,
I've a son called Idle Jack,
We live here in this village,
In a house like a bicycle rack.

Some people seemed surprised
So I'd better just explain,
How I came to come by
This most unusual name.

I'm a Pheasant plucker's daughter,
By a Pheasant plucker's son,
I also pluck Pheasants,
from dawn to setting sun.

Pheasant plucking's easy, plucking feathers by the score,
The worst thing about it, it makes your plucking fingers sore.

Enter Princess and Idol Jack.

Princess — I was just saying to Jack,
The lawns are not very green,
He'd better go and water them,
Or he's sure to upset the Queen.

Two square miles of lawn
Must be difficult to maintain,
But if he doesn't water it soon,
He'd better pray for rain.

Jack — Your Highness, it's too much,
Particularly for just one man,
Even if he had a garden hose,
And not just a watering can.

Stuff the Queen is what I say,
Though she may rant and rage,
Stuff her every orifice,
With onion and with sage.

Mother P — That's not the way to talk,
Son, show a little manners,
Even though the wicked bitch,
Has a face like a bag of spanners.

Princess — Mrs. Plucker, don't say those things,
For that, there is no call,
I know she can be difficult,
But she's my Mother after all.

Mother P — Sorry love, I got carried away,
Now Jack stop wasting time,
You'd get much more work done,
If you were up before half past nine.

Jack — I'm off now anyway,
I'll be gone before you say knives,
I'm taking the King his girly book,
He likes looking at Reader's Wives.

Enter the Queen – shouting.

Queen — Come on you lot,
Less talk, more elbow grease,
Jack go and do some gardening,
Or your employment here will cease.

I've never known anyone so idle,
You're too young to be put out to grass,
We'd probably get more life out of you,
If I put batteries up your Khyber Pass.

Jack — I'm going now Your Majesty,
I'm taking the King his books,
He can then amuse himself,
Whilst at Reader's Wives he looks.

Jack leaves.

Queen — Now then Mrs. Plucker,
I tell you that I've got a hunch,
That someone else will cook dinner,
If you're late serving lunch.

Mother P — Alright then Your Majesty,
I'll go to the kitchen right now,
And there I shall prepare luncheon,
(Aside) I hope it chokes the noisy cow.

Mother Plucker leaves.

Queen — It's your turn now young Jenny,
From me you'll get no quarter,
Your Father is too soft with you,
Because you're his only daughter.

Get on that spinning wheel,
Don't leave it before one o' clock,
Spin me some wonderful fabric,
From which I can make a nice frock.

Princess — *(Crying)* Oh Mummy, to me you are rotten,
I don't think you love me a lot,
Because I'm young and beautiful,
All of the things you're not.

Enter the King.

King — What is going on here then?
Tell me at once I demand,
Come, let me hold you my precious,
You're alright, I've just washed my hands.

I can't bear to see you cry,
It makes me angry and mean,
I want to take it out of someone,
Incidentally, seen my S & M Magazine?

Queen — You and your dirty books,
You men are all alike,
I much prefer to be with women,
But then that's why I'm a dyke.

King	Look, we agreed years ago, You go your way, I go mine, Just leave the Princess out of it, Or you'll be banished – from this pantomime.
Princess	Please don't fight over me, Why don't you two unite? Then all of us can be happy, By the way Mummy, what's a dyke?
Queen	That is none of your business, Listen to my point of view, Everything here was just rosy, Until I gave birth to you.
King	What a horrible thing to say, Upsetting my dear little mouse, I'm going to have to relieve this stress, Where's my copy of this months Penthouse?
Princess	Don't go just yet Daddy, I need to talk to you, In any case, when you go with your books, No-one else can get in the loo.

King — Sorry darling, I can't stop now,
I've got urgent things to do,
Now I've got my magazine,
I hope no-one's in the Loo.

When I've finished in there,
I'll have to empty the bucket,
It's always me that gets that job,
One day I'm going to say – blow it.

But first I'll chase Mother Plucker,
Around the kitchen table,
Then I'll get my leg across ,
Assuming I'm still able.

King leaves.

Queen — Now that he's gone my girl,
Get on that spinning wheel,
Be careful handling the needle,
Or a little prick you'll feel.

(To Audience) Little does the fool suspect,
In fact she has no fears,
That when the needle does draw blood,
She won't feel another prick for years.

You see I've poisoned the needle,
In her bloodstream the toxins will creep,
First of all she'll go drowsy,
Then fall in a deep, deep, sleep.

The Queen laughs loudly, then leaves.

Princess Jenny goes to the spinning wheel, and spins.

Princess — Oh gosh, I'm so sad,
I wish a Prince would come
And take me away from all this
Oops, I've just pricked my thumb.

My, I've suddenly gone sleepy,
I'll have to lie down on the bed,
I'll dream of a handsome Prince coming,
Who'll carry me away to wed.

Princess yawns, lies down and sleeps.

ACT TWO

Princess Jenny is still sleeping, and her family are gathered around her bed.

King
Two years now she's been asleep,
I'm worried about Princess Jenny,
You'd think that she would have to wake,
If only to spend a penny.

Queen
I know that you're terribly concerned,
It's only natural my dear,
But one thing you have to admit,
It's been lovely and quiet in here.

King
You're right, I am concerned,
I think perhaps we oughta,
Send for some-one who might know,
What's best for my darling daughter.

Queen
Forget about the wretched child,
She's nothing but a pampered brat,
And you with your weeping and wailing,
Are acting like perfect prize prat!

King — You've never liked the child,
In fact I'm prepared to bet,
That you had a hand in her falling asleep,
If so, I'll get at you yet.

I'll take away the things that you like,
Your whip and your black leather suits,
Your tattoo transfers, your nipple rings,
Your vibrator and Doc. Martin boots.

Queen — You keep your hands away from my things,
Love your daughter as much as you please,
But take one step towards my bondage equip'
And I'll cut off your wrinkled testes.

King — That would suit you very well,
For something more than a crown
That you've always wanted,
Is a pair of balls of your own.

Enter Mother Plucker.

Mother P — Excuse me both Your Highnesses,
But there's someone here at the door,
He's asked if you can give him ten minutes,
And it's not the Avon Lady, for sure.

Queen As long as it's not Jehovah's Witnesses,
Or any of that Mormon tribe,
For the way they keep banging on,
Is one thing I can't abide.

Mother P No he's not any of them,
I can tell from the way that he's dressed,
The only thing they have in common,
Is that this lad looks to be well blessed.

King Alright then, show him in,
I've got time for a very short chat,
If he should be selling things,
I'll try to knock off the V.A.T.

Mother P I'll go and bring him in,
His attributes seem to be many,
Perhaps while he's in this room,
He'll know how to wake Princess Jenny.

Mother Plucker leaves.

Queen We'll continue this argument later,
In an hour I've got a date,
As she's a Vicar's daughter,
I'm expecting it there on a plate.

King — Begone you old queer forever,
Don't darken my doorstep again,
And may every human that you ever meet,
Be heterosexual men.

Queen — I'm going, don't you worry,
You're only good for lavatorial chores,
I say this to you and your daughter,
Good-bye, good riddance, UP YOURS!

Queen storms out.

Enter Mother Plucker, Idle Jack and the Prince.

Mother P — This is the man, Your Majesty,
You'll agree it's no idle boast,
To say that he's tall and handsome,
And bulges where it matters most.

Idle Jack — I could have a figure like that,
But exercise is needed – it's said,
That being the case, I've made my choice,
I'd rather be lying in bed.

Prince — Sire, let me introduce myself,
I'm a Prince from a nearby estate,
My family has fallen on hard times,
That's what brings me to your castle gate.

	So that I can earn a living, I sell flags and other regalia, And whilst doing this, I heard the sad tale, Of the lovely Princess Jenny Tallia.
Idle Jack	Never mind the Princess, My Mother will look after her, Why not help me in the garden, But you'll do the bigger share.
King	Hang on just a minute Jack, Prince, your demeanour seems kind, When you came knocking on my door, What exactly had you in mind?
Prince	First, if I could see the girl, Then help her to open her eyes, I'll do some kissing and fondling, So you may hear heavy breathing and sighs.
Idle Jack	Do you think he can be trusted, Kissing and cuddling our Jenny? In all the years that I've worked here, I've never managed to get any.

Mother P I believe the King is right,
We can trust in his good name,
But if he should do her any harm,
He'll go home with two things less than he came.

King Carry on Prince, do what you can,
Make sure that you don't go too far,
If you're thinking of loosening things,
I can tell you, she's not wearing a bra.

The Prince goes to Princess Jenny and starts to kiss and fondle her.

Idle Jack Look at him, the dirty swine,
Doing that and acting so bold,
Doing the things I've wanted to,
Ever since I was fourteen years old.

Look at him now, it can't be right,
For her purity I'm starting to fear,
One hand on that, the other on there,
And his tongue has now entered her ear.

Mother P Look! Look! She's beginning to stir,
I'm feeling excited myself,
It's all so very erotic,
Like a video off the top shelf.

King
I know exactly what you mean,
I'm almost too embarrassed to look,
But if it goes on much longer,
I'll have to go to the loo with a book.

The Princess awakes and sits up.

Princess
My oh my that was wonderful,
And to wake up is such a relief,
Who is this smiling stranger
With pubic hair stuck to his teeth?

It's lovely to see you again Daddy,
And you Mrs. P. and you Jack,
It's even nicer to sit up,
Having spent two years on my back.

Prince
Princess Jenny you're more lovely,
Than the moon and the stars in the sky,
You can see how much you excite me,
If you just glance down at my fly.

Princess
Oh young Sire really you shouldn't,
I am the King's daughter you know.
Although I must say it's amusing,
To sit here and watch your love grow.

Mother P — What a lovely young couple,
The Prince, and the beautiful Princess,
If they should decide to get married,
Perhaps the King will buy me a new dress.

King — I'll do more than that Mrs. Plucker,
For now that I'm here on my own,
The dress that I'm going to buy you,
Will be your own wedding gown.

Mother P — Are you saying that we're to get married?
Is that what you really mean?
If that's the case I'm honoured,
For I shall be the next Queen.

Prince — Congratulations to you both,
It's a marriage that's made in Heaven,
She has the body, and you have the cash,
You could honeymoon in… Devon.

That is what I'd like to do,
If the Princess will marry a pauper,
I'll have to sell lots of bunting and flags,
To be able to feed your daughter.

King — Let's all get married together,
And let no time be lost,
We'll do it next Saturday,
As there's four, it may cut the cost.

Prince	Well that is great news Sire, For the Princess and I will be wed, We shan't be attending the reception, As from the church we'll go straight to bed.
Idle Jack	It's all good news for you four, But there's one thing I have to say, While you lot are getting married, I'll have no part to play.
King	Don't worry about that Jack, Our wedding plans are all laid, They are the brides, we are the grooms, You'll be best man and bridesmaid.

END

Goldilocks

THE CAST

Goldilocks	A young blonde virgin, who's only similarity to a jumbo jet is that they both have a black box.
Puck	King of the wood fairies. Rather sensitive as he thinks he keeps hearing people tell him to go away.
Fairy	Puck's companion whose interests include macramé and writing letters to Playboy magazine.
Granny	A right slag who will screw anyone, try anything, and doesn't mind having her photograph taken doing it – somewhat like the Duchess of York.
The Wolf	An ignorant animal with no knowledge of other animals in the wood. When asked what a Fox was, replied it was something you do on the second date.

ACT ONE

Scene opens with Goldilocks alone in the woods, and she is crying.

Goldilocks

Oh my, I'm so sad,
Will no-one pity me?
For I am all alone,
No friends for company.

I think that I'm attractive,
My figure is now full grown,
Can anyone tell me then,
Why I've no boyfriend of my own?

I am just seventeen,
My innocence not yet gone,
I've been trying to get laid
Since I've had hair I could sit upon.

Why won't some young man
Drink from my flowing cup?
If I have to wait much longer,
I'm afraid I might heal up.

She cries – enter the Wood Fairies.

Puck Hello, my name is Puck,
That's spelt P.U.C.K.
I'm King of all the Fairies,
But in no way am I gay.

We overheard your story,
It's such an awful plight,
We'll put on our thinking caps,
And try to put things right.

Fairy In the woods there lives a woodsman,
Aged somewhere in his teens,
Handsome, tall and witty,
With a big bulge in his jeans.

I'm sure that he's not spoken for,
And now then when I think,
I've never seen him with a girl,
And doesn't he dress in pink?

Puck No, No, you stupid fool,
You're thinking of Jack Horner,
He's the one that sits alone,
And plays with himself in a corner.

Surely it's Boy Blue you mean,
He hangs around Bo Peep,
He doesn't know who he fancies most,
The girl, or one of her sheep.

Fairy — I remember it now,
This fellows name is Jack,
He tends to fall down a lot,
And gave poor Jill the clap.

He's totally cured now,
Of that there is no doubt,
He's masculine and muscular,
Built like a brick shithouse.

He'll make an ideal partner,
And as far as thrills go,
He'll give you all that you desire,
If not....I'd buy a black dildo.

Goldilocks — Let's go and find him,
Then perhaps may be,
Having seen my eager body,
He'll surely fancy me.

We'll fool around a little,
Our hands will start to run
Over each others best bits,
Then we'll start to have some fun.

Puck — Hang on just a minute,
The details you can skimp,
Or we'll be so excited,
We'll start to walk with a limp.

Goldilocks Oh I'm so sorry lads,
But for this I've waited so long,
For someone handsome and muscular,
And please God… also well hung.

Puck Well let us go and find him,
This handsome fellow called Jack,
And if he's in working order,
We'll try to bring him back.

Goldilocks I'm sorry I can't go with you,
I have to visit my Gran.
But as soon as I have finished,
I'll come and look at this man.

If he's as good as you tell me,
I'll be very grateful, and more,
One day a month I'll meet you,
When each of you can score.

Fairy That's good enough for me Puck,
At the thought of it, I'm getting heady,
And as you see from the front of my pants,
I'm very excited already.

Puck Take your hands out of your pockets,
You must be out of your mind,
If you don't break that habit,
You're in danger of going blind.

Goldilocks Right then, I'm off now,
You boys are far too rude,
I'm going to my Grans house,
And I'm taking her some food.

I'll take her lots of goodies,
With fruit my basket I'll pack,
And while I'm handling the bananas
I'll be thinking of young Jack.

Puck We're going to see the three bears,
Who live here in the wood,
Their porridge may taste lousy,
But their beds are pretty good.

Cheerio – see you later,
Have yourself a lovely time,
You can tell us all about it
If we're still in this Pantomime.

We've not read Act Two script yet,
Which seems a shame and pity,
But for now we'll say goodbye,
By singing you this ditty.......

Puck and the Fairy sing to the tune of 'The Teddybear's Picnic'.

If you go down to the woods today
You're sure of a big surprise,
If you go down to the woods today
You'd better just close your eyes,
For every bear that ever there was
Is getting his share today because
Today's the day the Teddybears wet their
dipstick.....

Nookie time for Teddybears,
The Teddybears are getting it away today,
Mustn't catch them unawares
Heterosexual, Lesbian and some are gay,
See them gaily jump and hump,
They love to hump and jump while spitting
out pubic hairs,
At 6 am they'll all get up and go home to
their beds,
Because they are shagged out Teddybears.

ACT TWO

Granny's cottage. Granny and the Wolf have just finished making love....

Granny — Ah! That was wonderful Wolfie
In fact it was simply great,
I haven't had a jump as good as that
Since I was sixty eight.

Your technique was almost perfect,
Your rhythm was so divine,
The fur on your belly, turned my knees to jelly,
Particularly when it passed over my spine.

Wolf — Well thank you Granny baby,
For an old one you did just fine,
I must say, you're a hell of a lay
And we must do it again sometime.

The reason I give satisfaction,
I'm sure Riding Hood would tell,
It's not just my eyes, mouth and teeth that are large,
But my private parts as well.

Granny	Whatever the reason, I love it,
I want it from night until dawn,
Can we now do Doggie fashion?
But in here and not on the lawn.

Wolf	Hang on a while you old nympho,
You're working me half to death,
We'll do it again in a minute
As soon as I get back my breath.

I want to do something different,
So my perverted mind I will probe,
Stand on your head with your legs in the air
And I'll dive off the wardrobe.

Granny	I'll rub all over my body,
My skin will have a bright sheen,
But instead of using baby oil,
I'll apply some wintergreen.

Granny	You'll take Champagne and Oysters,
To help you perform again,
To give me the necessary kick start,
I'll drink some Sanatagen.

Wolf	Just a minute Petal,
My big ears just heard a knock,
I'll go and see who's at the door
If you'll pass me my other sock.

Granny — I wonder who it can be
It's certainly given me a fright,
It can't be kids collecting money
As it's not yet Bonfire night.

Wolf — I can open the door now
That I've got on both of my socks,
Well look who it is, what a surprise
It's your grand-daughter, Goldilocks.

Goldilocks pokes her head around the door, and speaks to the Wolf.

Goldilocks — Goodness sakes who are you?
And what's that thing rising so sudden?
I've never seen one as big as that,
It reminds me, I must get a black pudding.

Granny — Come inside Goldilocks,
Don't stand there outside,
This is my friend, the Big Bad Wolf
Who's served me since your Grand-dad died

Wolf — That's right little baby,
Don't wait out there any longer,
Come inside and up the stairs
I fancy something a bit younger.

Granny — Yes, come my little darling,
Today you can become a star,
Three in a bed together,
I've never tried a menage a trois.

Goldilocks — Your offer sounds so tempting,
But it's come a day too late,
I've found myself a boyfriend,
His love will compensate.

Although we've not met yet,
He'll give me all I need,
Jack and I are compatible
And his manly lust I'll feed.

Granny — What a load of cobblers,
You're being far too fussy,
Come and play with us two Cats,
And we will stroke your pussy.

Wolf — That's right chicken, come and play,
Forget about your Jack,
In the love making stakes,
I'm the leader of the pack.

Goldilocks — No! No! I don't want to,
Please now let me go,
You're hurting my arm quite badly,
I bruise very easily you know.

Help! Help! Oh please help me,
I'm calling my friends of the wood,
Whether they're Bears or Fairies
If they help, I promise to be good.

No more will I tease Humpty Dumpty,
Making him fall off the wall,
Noddy and Big Ears can play safely,
And I won't talk dirty at all.

Wolf — Stop your row you stupid woman,
Your screams must be abated
Or your Granny will go to jail,
And I'm likely to be castrated.

Goldilocks — No, No, I won't stop,
Can anyone hear me out there?
Any of the Fairies of the wood,
Jack, or Rupert Bear?

Puck — *(Voice off)* Alright Goldilocks, we're coming
To save you from that so and so,
We'll make sure they release you
So that you leave here 'intacto'

Puck and Fairy rush into the room.

Fairy Let go of her you two perverts,
You see we like her so much
That we're prepared to do you harm,
And kick you both in the crutch.

Wolf No please don't do that,
Pain to me is a no-no,
Besides I want to father cubs,
And I don't want to sing soprano.

Granny Don't try that on me laddie,
I want to make it quite clear,
If you should kick me in that spot,
Your boots likely to disappear.

Wolf Come on old'un let us run,
Now seems the appropriate time,
We've turned out to be the baddies
In this bloody Pantomime.

Granny and Wolf run off stage.

Goldilocks Thank you friendly fairies
For saving my good name,
For if I'd joined them in their fun
They'd soon have me on the game.

Puck All's well that ends well,
Go home to Jack and reality,
While you do, the Bears and us
Will indulge in bestiality.

With that we end our story,
We'll finish with a song,
If you happen to know the chorus,
Why not sing along.

All sing to the tune of "We're Busy Doing Nothin'"

We're busy screwin' Bruin
Screwin' the whole day through
Trying to find a position that's totally new
We'd like to hump Teddy and also Rupert Bear
We'd also bugger Sooty, if Corbett's hand wasn't there.
La La La La La La La La La La...

We hope you liked our story
Although it wasn't clean,
Hope you didn't find it in anyway too obscene,
If we did offend you with our tale of

Goldilocks,
We'd say farewell, and go to hell, and add to that... BOLLOCKS
La La La La La La La La La La …………

All leaves stage, waving.

END

* 9 7 8 1 7 8 0 3 5 4 1 2 5 *
ND - #0156 - 050826 - C0 - 197/132/8 [10] - CB - 9781780354125 - Gloss Lamination